BEAUTIFUL FLORAL BOUQUETS

TO PAINT OR COLOR

Charlene Tarbox

DOVER PUBLICATIONS, INC.
Mineola, New York

In Memory of Opal

Note

This vibrant assortment of floral bouquets includes some charming arrangements of blooming flowers, sprays tied with ribbon, and other exquisite cut flowers artfully displayed in ornate vases and decorative pitchers. These elegant and finely detailed illustrations of irises, roses, daisies, daffodils, and other delightful favorites are ideal for use in any arts and crafts project. Simply add your own color to bring these images of blossoms to stunning life.

Artist Charlene Tarbox has brilliantly captured the graceful beauty of floral bouquets in full bloom. The 23 plates in this book are perforated for easy removal and are printed on one side only, so dark markers and paints will not show through. In addition, the outlines have been printed in a light gray line so that they virtually disappear when painted or colored, resulting in a more polished and professional appearance.

Bibliographical Note

Beautiful Floral Bouquets to Paint or Color is a new work, first published by Dover Publications, Inc., in 2006.

International Standard Book Number

ISBN-13: 978-0-486-44932-6
ISBN-10: 0-486-44932-7

Manufactured in the United States by LSC Communications
44932707   2018
www.doverpublications.com